Francis Drake

by David Goodnough
illustrated by Burt Dodson

Troll Associates

Troll Associates, Mahwah, N.J.
Library of Congress Catalog Card Number: 78-18056
ISBN 0-89375-173-1
ISBN 0-89375-165-0 Paper Edition

10   9   8   7   6   5   4   3   2

Francis Drake

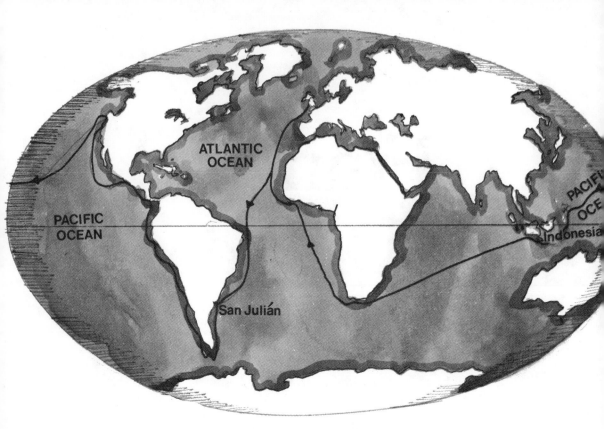

ATLANTIC
OCEAN

PACIFIC
OCEAN

PACIFIC
OCEAN

Indonesia

San Julián

Drake's Voyage

On December 13, 1577, a fleet of five ships sailed from the harbor of Plymouth, England. Usually, when a fleet left the harbor, it was like a holiday in the town. Church bells rang, hymns were sung by the sailors aboard the ships, townspeople cheered wildly from the shore. But this fleet, under the command of Captain Francis Drake, left quietly, almost secretly.

The crew and the townspeople had been told that the ships were sailing to the Mediterranean Sea to trade in North Africa. The people of Plymouth were not fooled, however. Captain Drake had already earned a reputation as a daring "sea dog"—a captain who fearlessly raided the ports and vessels of the two powerful seafaring nations, Spain and Portugal. Everyone knew that wherever Drake sailed, there would be adventure—and the chance for great wealth.

6

Francis Drake paced the deck of his flagship, the *Pelican*, and easily guided the fleet out of the harbor and into the English Channel. He had sailed these waters for most of his life. The son of a poor farmer, he had gone to sea at the age of ten.

After only a few years as an ordinary seaman, Drake had become a ship's captain for John Hawkins, his cousin. Hawkins came from a very powerful and wealthy family. He had become even wealthier by trading with the Spanish colonies of South and Central America.

Drake had red hair and a bright red beard. His eyes were blue, and he was known for his cool, steady gaze. The men who sailed with Drake had learned to fear that gaze—and his queen, Elizabeth I, had learned to respect it.

On this chilly morning, Drake was heading his ships toward the Pacific Ocean—where no English ships had ever sailed before. Many years earlier, Spain and Portugal had both claimed lands newly discovered in America. To avoid war with each other, the two countries had agreed to divide the world in half for purposes of trading and discovering new lands.

Spain was given the western half of the globe, which included most of America and the Pacific Ocean. Portugal was given the other half, which included Africa, the East Indies, and all the undiscovered lands of Asia.

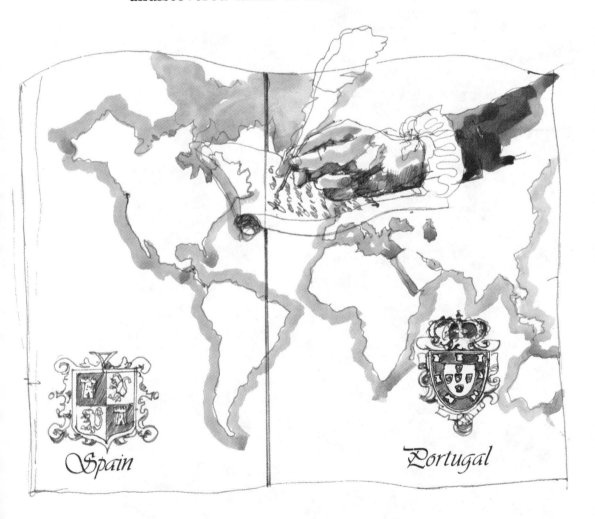

Spain

Portugal

Other seafaring countries, such as Holland and England, were given nothing in this agreement. They were not considered important enough to have a share of the wealth taken from new lands.

But many English sea captains, like John Hawkins and Francis Drake, paid no attention to the agreement. Year after year, they risked their lives by sailing the Spanish waters of the Atlantic Ocean. They traded in Spanish-owned ports, and even attacked Spanish vessels. Although Queen Elizabeth officially could not approve of what they were doing, she secretly supported them. She even provided money and ships, and shared in the treasures these daring men brought back.

Today, as he called out orders to his crew, Drake thought of another voyage. Five years earlier, he had boldly sailed into Panama. There, he had not only captured several Spanish ships—he had also taken a mule train, loaded with silver from Peru. After his victory, a friendly Indian had taken him aside and pointed to a tall tree at the top of a hill. A platform had been built high in its branches. Drake climbed up to this lookout and gazed at an amazing sight.

Below him stretched the narrow green Isthmus of Panama. To the west were the waters of the vast Pacific Ocean. What a sight to behold! This was the Great South Sea that every Englishman had heard about—but few had seen.

Drake stared for a long while. Then he smiled. "So the Spanish think this is all theirs, do they? Well, some day *I* will sail that sea."

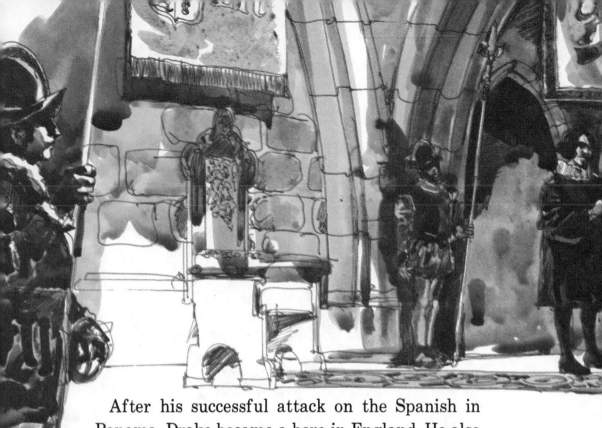

After his successful attack on the Spanish in Panama, Drake became a hero in England. He also made himself a wealthy man. Queen Elizabeth herself had asked to meet him.

At court, Drake told the queen that great riches could be gained from the mines of Peru and Mexico. He also told her of his secret plans. "Your Majesty, if I am allowed to sail into the Great South Sea to strike at Spanish treasure ships, this will not only weaken Spain—it will make England rich."

16

The queen nodded. She knew that England needed money. She could not even afford a fleet to defend her country. There were other reasons for sending ships into this great ocean. Perhaps they would discover new lands for England. Drake might even find the Northwest Passage—the waterway that Europeans believed connected the Atlantic and Pacific Oceans.

The queen was convinced, and an agreement was made. Elizabeth and her noblemen would invest in Drake's voyage. But the queen's part in it was to remain forever a secret. Spies for the king of Spain were everywhere—Drake's mission must be hidden from them. If he failed, he must take his secret with him to the bottom of the sea.

Now Drake, with five ships, was bound for the Great South Sea. Favorable winds took the ships southward. Off the coast of Africa, Drake lost no time in capturing a Portuguese cargo vessel. Drake was known to be one of the best navigators of his time. Whenever he captured a ship, he went first to its chartroom. There he examined the charts and navigational instruments—and took those he thought were better than his own.

Drake's fleet left the coast of Africa and headed west into the waters of the Atlantic Ocean. But instead of following the usual course to the West Indies, Drake turned south. After several days of sailing, the crew and the soldiers aboard became alarmed. They began to mutter among themselves.

Where were they going? What was their mission? Were they going to trade? To discover new lands? Or to fight the Spaniards?

They did not know it then, but they were going to do all these things—and more!

By the time the fleet had almost reached the Strait of Magellan near the tip of South America, the mood of the men had grown worse. Drake had to restore order. He had to convince the crews and any noblemen aboard the ships that he, and he alone, was their commander.

There were whispers of a planned mutiny. But after Drake found out about it, he acted quickly. When the fleet stopped for supplies at San Julián, in Argentina, he arrested the leader of the plot and had him executed.

After this, Drake called all his men together. He told them about the dangerous mission they were on. He hinted of the queen's confidence in them, and spoke of the importance of their success. He warned that he would permit absolutely no disobedience. From then on, Drake had no more trouble with his crews.

It was now more than eight months since they had left England. At San Julián, Drake had ordered the two small supply ships, which were old and in poor condition, to be unloaded and destroyed. He knew that the journey ahead would be difficult.

24

In August, 1578, the three remaining ships passed through the dangerous Strait of Magellan with little trouble. But as the tiny fleet came out of the Strait, the ships were suddenly struck by a furious storm. One ship, the *Marigold*, was overturned by the howling winds, and all aboard were drowned. The *Elizabeth* was blown far off course, and finally had to return to England.

The *Pelican*, Drake's flagship, was left alone in the Great South Sea. But Captain Drake had no thoughts of turning back. He renamed his ship the *Golden Hind*—after the golden deer on the coat of arms of a nobleman. The nobleman had invested much money in the voyage. Now it was up to this ship alone to complete the mission.

A storm drove the ship southward into open water for a short time. But soon the weather became calm, and Drake headed north. His task was to raid the Spanish-held colonies along the coast. At one point, he sailed a small boat into a harbor to gather food and fresh water. The Indians who gathered to watch seemed friendly—until the boat reached the sandy beach. Then they showered it with arrows. Drake was wounded, and four of his men were killed. The rest barely escaped with their lives.

Drake knew from experience that most of the Indians of South America hated the Spanish conquerors, and there was no way for them to know that the *Golden Hind* was not a Spanish ship.

Drake continued to sail up the coast until he spied a large Spanish galleon. The Spanish captain did not have any reason to be suspicious of the small ship that rapidly overtook him. Before he knew it, his decks were swarming with English seamen swinging swords! Taken completely by surprise, the captain soon surrendered.

One of the Spanish sailors jumped overboard and swam ashore to warn the nearby town. The townspeople fled to the hills, leaving everything behind. Drake went ashore and helped himself to all the food he needed. Then he stripped the Spanish ship of all that was worth taking. The ship was carrying a large amount of gold and precious jewels.

Afterward, Drake sailed the *Golden Hind* into a sheltered bay. Here he ordered his crew to scrape the barnacles from the hull. These shellfish grew in great numbers on the bottom of ships and eventually slowed them down. Next, Drake ordered his large guns brought up from the hold and mounted on the deck. A smaller ship, called a *pinnace*, had been taken apart and stored below deck. It was now taken out and put together again. It would sail alongside the *Golden Hind*.

Now they were ready for anything!

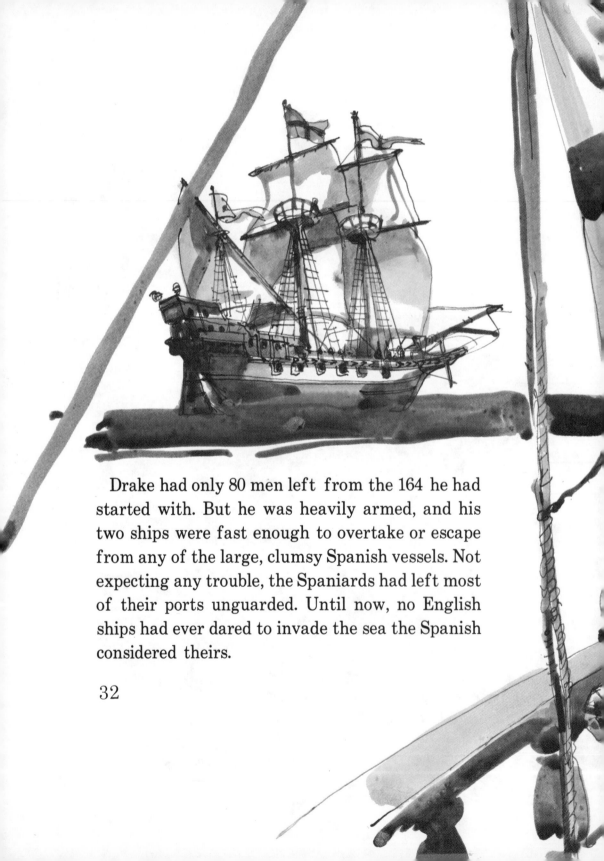

Drake had only 80 men left from the 164 he had started with. But he was heavily armed, and his two ships were fast enough to overtake or escape from any of the large, clumsy Spanish vessels. Not expecting any trouble, the Spaniards had left most of their ports unguarded. Until now, no English ships had ever dared to invade the sea the Spanish considered theirs.

32

So far, Drake's luck had been good. He had captured many ships and had filled his flagship with gold and silver and jewels. But he was still searching for the big prize—a fully loaded treasure ship.

Shortly after Drake crossed the equator, he sighted a large Spanish galleon. A cannon shot into its rigging brought down one of the masts. Sailors from the *Golden Hind* leaped aboard from one side, while men from the pinnace boarded from the other.

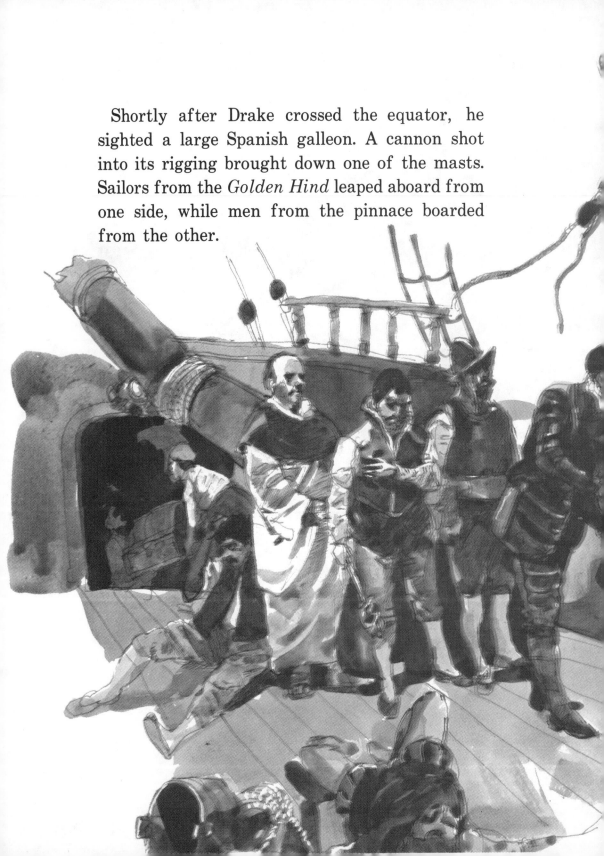

When Drake inspected the captured ship, he found that it contained enough treasure to pay for his whole voyage—including his lost ships. There would even be enough left over to provide a large profit for the queen and the other investors.

Drake now transferred all the treasure to the *Golden Hind* and let the Spanish ship go. Then he set a northerly course. He hoped to find the Northwest Passage, which would allow his ships to sail eastward, back into the Atlantic Ocean.

Drake continued sailing along almost the whole western coast of North America, going as far as Vancouver Island, in Canada. But he did not find any waterway to the east.

Turning the ship southward again, Drake entered a bay just north of what is now the city of San Francisco. The *Golden Hind* was leaking and had to be repaired. The treasure was brought up from her hold and stored in a rough fort.

Drake claimed the land in the name of Queen Elizabeth, calling it New Albion, after the ancient name for England. The white cliffs along the coast of California reminded him of the southern coast of England, where he had sailed so often as a boy.

To make his claim official, Drake scratched a few words on a brass plate and nailed it to a tree near the bay. He also nailed a coin to the plate. On it was the queen's picture and her coat of arms.

Now Drake had to decide how he would return to England. If he sailed back the way he had come, he knew Spanish warships would be waiting for him. The *Golden Hind* was now a floating storehouse of jewels, gold, and silver. It was as heavy and clumsy as the large ships he would have to avoid.

So Drake headed west. He would cross the Pacific and Indian Oceans.

His passage to the Philippine Islands was an easy one. From the Philippines, he sailed south toward the islands of Indonesia. In the past, only Portugal had been permitted to trade for the rich spices found in these islands. But many Islanders did not like the Portuguese. With plenty of gold to pay for spices, Drake soon made trading agreements.

Then, knowing his long voyage was near a triumphant end, he happily set his course for England.

On September 26, 1580, the *Golden Hind* sailed into Plymouth Harbor. It had been almost three years since she had slipped quietly out into the English Channel. Francis Drake had become the first commander to sail around the world. . .and live to tell about it. The great navigator Ferdinand Magellan of Portugal had been killed before his fleet returned from his round-the-world voyage 60 years earlier.

But for Drake, there was another reason to rejoice. He had made England rich. With the treasure he had brought back, Queen Elizabeth would be able to raise an army and build a fleet of warships to protect England from the powerful Spaniards. And she now had valuable trading rights in the East Indies — which would be one of Drake's greatest gifts to his country. Trading companies would be formed, and English colonies would be started around the world. England would soon become a great empire.

43

When the king of Spain learned of Drake's conquests, he was furious. He demanded that Elizabeth put Drake to death as a pirate. Instead, the queen ordered Drake to bring the *Golden Hind* to London.

44

As Queen Elizabeth stepped aboard the ship, Francis Drake knelt before her. She took the sword of one of her noblemen, and said with a smile, "My dear pirate—the king of Spain has asked for your head. Now I will have it." Then she lightly touched his shoulder with the sword. *"Arise, Sir Francis Drake!"*

The queen honored Drake with knighthood for his bold conquests of Spanish treasure ships and ports in the Pacific. In so doing, Elizabeth so enraged the king of Spain that he declared war on England not long afterward.

In May, 1588, Spain sent more than 130 warships to invade England. Sir Francis Drake, now a vice admiral, had an important part in the great naval battle that took place in the English Channel. The Royal Navy succeeded in sinking many Spanish vessels. Defeated, the remaining ships in the once-mighty "Invincible Armada"— the *unbeatable fleet*—fled. Now England had proved itself a major sea power.

Drake continued to serve his country and his queen. But he was never very long away from the sea. And it was at sea that he died.

In January, 1596, during a voyage in the West Indies, Sir Francis Drake died of a tropical disease. He was buried at sea—in the same waters where he had first gained fame as England's greatest and most daring seaman.